REFOCUSING
THE AFRICAN-AMERICAN
DREAM

A Personal, Professional, and
Human Perspective of Two Twins'
Dreams, Hope, and Passion

Edwin E. Thompson RIA, MBA
MSgt. Edward E. Thompson, Jr. USAF (Ret.)

authorHOUSE®

AuthorHouse™
1663 Liberty Drive
Bloomington, IN 47403
www.authorhouse.com
Phone: 1 (800) 839-8640

Published by AuthorHouse 05/13/2020

ISBN: 978-1-7283-6184-0 (sc)
ISBN: 978-1-7283-6183-3 (e)

Library of Congress Control Number: 2020908725

Print information available on the last page.

This book is printed on acid-free paper.

DEDICATION

This book is dedicated to our grandmother the late Izetta Graham
1907 to 2007
And
Our mother Orzie Lene Thompson
1934 to 2020
From the words of her great grandson on
June 30, 2007, at her homegoing
Travaris J. Striggles, Sr.
Yes, we gather here today to pay our respects and pray. Let there be
sunshine among us, even when clouds are gray. It behooves us to know
our Lord and Savior and stay far, far away from ill-gotten behavior.
Now, grandmother, Izetta lived to be 100 years
old. And I declare that to be a blessing,
God bless her soul a century it was meant to be.
It's shortly thereafter eventually the Lord came and shown his
face and said, rest in my arms you have run your race.
You said your grace in reverence to others around you.
This is a testimony of what you are and is what you will be.
We love you, and we will miss you. Rest In Heaven-Amen.

CONTENTS

THE THOMPSON'S TWINS

MY PEOPLE

WHAT CAN I DO

1. INTRODUCTION

"This book depicts the challenging experiences of two twins-Dreams, Hope, and Passion in obtaining the American Dream." First, we must establish the Argument for Refocusing the African American Dream; and review the implications of MLK "I Have A Dream" Speech. Secondly, we must recap the success and failures of both twins and Thirdly, is the Dreams, Hope, and Passion premise real or can it be used as a template for obtaining personal success.

1.1. What is Freedom?

Establishing the argument for *"Refocusing the African American Dream"* is precipitated by the need to clarify what is freedom, and what makes freedom so important? Great thinkers, politicians, writers, and artists have debated the meaning of freedom throughout history. (Archibald Maceishnd.) describes, *"Freedom is the right to choose: the right to create for yourself the alternatives of choice. Without the possibility of choice and the exercise of choice, a man is not a man but a member, an instrument, a thing ".* [1] However, Bernard Malamute states freedom, as *"The purpose of freedom is to create it for others."* Edward R. Morrow states, *"We cannot defend freedom abroad by deserting it at home."* [2]

---

[1] Archibald MacLeish. (n.d.). Retrieved 4 13, 2020, from Poetry Foundation:

[2] https://www.goodreads.com/author/quotes/178884.Edward_R_Murrow Alternatives(October 27)-WordPoints. https://wordpoints.com/alternatives -october-27/

What is the Price of Freedom?

On the other hand, the Declaration of Independence depicts the concept of freedom in terms of inalienable rights, liberty, and the pursuit of happiness as the hallmark of a free society, and lastly, Thomas Jefferson declarative statement states, *"The price of freedom is eternal vigilance. "* This vigilance is necessary because life is a continuous stream. Only through continued vigilance can "We the People" preserve our way of freedom, which allows us the opportunity to pursue and realized *"The American Dream."* We the People need to be reminded occasionally, that unimaginable pain, suffering has paid for that freedom we all enjoy James Toulow Adams first used the phrase *"The American Dream"* in his 1934 book the Epic of America. [3] He states:

The American Dream is "that dream of a land in which life should be better and richer and fuller for everyone, with opportunity for each according to ability or achievement. It is a difficult dream for the European upper classes to interpret adequately, and too many of us ourselves have grown weary and mistrustful of it. It is not a dream of motor cars and high wages merely, but a dream of social order in which each man and each woman shall be able to attain to the fullest stature of which they are innately capable, and be recognized by others for what they are, regardless of the fortuitous circumstances of birth or position." (Pp. 214-215) [14] [5]

Since the 1963 March on Washington, D.C., and Martin Luther King's 'I Have a Dream Speech, the majority of Black America still have not realized *"The American Dream."* The following groups have had the most trouble in attaining "The American Dream": Native Americans, Irish Americans, Chinese Americans, and Japanese Americans, as well as the poor and

---

[3] Robinson, Morgan. "Thirst For The American Dream: The Lost City Of Flint 1." Michigan Sociological Review, vol. 32, Michigan Sociological Association, Oct. 2018, p. 170.

[4] Robinson, Morgan. "Thirst For The American Dream: The Lost City Of Flint 1." Michigan Sociological Review, vol. 32, Michigan Sociological Association, Oct. 2018, p. 170.

[5] *The Epic of America* (1931) https://en.wikipedia.org/wiki/James_Truslow_Adams#American_Dream

women. Based on the gravity of social issues confronting Black America, it appears that we, as people, have missed interpret MLK speech on the grounds of what is the true price of equality and freedom; with *"Freedom Comes Responsibility."*

The twin believes that the critical components of the *"American Dream"* can be fundamentally pursued through Dreams, Hope, and Passion. Generally, dreams are food for the soul. Dreams also give us hope. Whereas, hope is the opportunity for expectation, and passion is the need and desire to turn those hopes and dreams into reality. Our empirical knowledge and experiences support this belief. The objective of this book is not to focus on discussing all the intricacies of social problems surrounding "Black America," but to direct our attention primarily on the fundamental causes. The root cause approach requires us to place cause and effect in the context of where we need to go, in terms of realizing the "American Dream." We believe a broader picture consists of taking *"Personal Responsibility"* and fostering "Economic Independence." *Our lives are not determined by what happens to us, but how we react to what happens; not by what life brings to us, but by the attitude we bring to life. A positive attitude causes a chain reaction of positive thoughts, events, and outcomes. It is a catalyst, which generates extraordinary results (Author Unknown).* [6]

Key Societal Problems Facing Black America

There are three fundamental critical societal problems, which impacts "The African American Dream," they are fundamentally social problems notably: an increase in single-parent households, inadequate education preparation, and no economic foundation

---

[6] Our lives are not determined by what happens to us but by.... https://www.scrapbook.com/quotes/doc/5128.html **;** https://www.brainyquote.com/quotes/wade_boggs_311636

Single Family Household

The family structure is the most basic and ancient of all institutions, and it remains the fundamental social unit in every society. Yet there are many experts today who predict the end of the family system, as we know it. The family structure appears to be breaking down and is the victim of moral decay, sexual permissiveness, and changing gender roles. Such predictions are commonplace in many industrialized societies, but the statistics suggest that the family system of the world's leading industrial society, the United States, is under the greatest pressure. One in every five American births is to an unmarried mother, usually a teenager. One in every four pregnancies ends in an abortion, [7] and the current high school dropout rate appears to remain stable at 11 percent. Remember, nature is made up of two sexes: a male and a female. So, what makes humans so different. (Statistics, 2008). [8]

The Need for Education

However, inadequate education preparation is compounded by an increase in single-family households. Based on today's requirements, a high school diploma, vocational trade, or a college degree are a critical milestone for obtaining personal success. The individual gains of education are more obvious, but society also benefits from the skills and knowledge of an educated society. For today's high school students, a college education represents more than an opportunity for continued learning; it represents a vehicle for personal growth. The opportunity to increase one's economic status and personal independence, to pursue a career, is the foundation of the American dream. Education, ingenuity, and perseverance have always been an essential component for the quest to seeking the American Dream.

---

[7] John S. Feinberg & Paul D. Feinberg, Abortion – Perfectio https://horvathliviu. wordpress.com/2011/03/14/john-s-feinberg-paul-d-feinberg-abortion/

[8] https://horvathliviu.wordpress.com/2011/03/14/john-s-feinberg-paul-d-feinberg-abortion/

Poor or No Economic Foundation

Despite the problems associated with single-family households and inadequate education preparation. The last critical societal problem is no economic foundation. The Declaration of Independence depicts the concept of freedom in terms of inalienable rights, liberty, and the pursuit of happiness. As a result, there is no mention of economic independence. Economics is an important issue, which confronts our families; because it is a necessary means for financial independence, and it facilitates our participation in a market economy. The goal of many immigrants who came to this country over the last 100 years ago was not political power; it was an economic power. Political power is usually acquired through a structured party, run by clearly defined leaders, to meet mutually agreed-upon goals. People can join for political power under many different organizations and groups. You can be a member of a political party or an ideological constituency.[9] You can work toward your political means as a member of organizations such as the NAACP, Concerned Women for America, National Rifle Association, National Organization for Women, or your local church. However, It seems odd to us that "Arab Americans" and "Jewish Americans" with such vital and traditional political priorities appear to place more interest in the economics of America than politics whereas, many of our black social leaders appear to concentrate on political power. Since MLK's assassination, these leaders have been more interested in political power because it empowers them. On the other hand, if the individual is empowered, that individual will not need a leader. [10]This appears to be a significant focus of many black leaders since MLK's assassination, so therefore we have to focus on the power of economics versus political power. There is an exception to every rule. Most individuals do not operate under an exception to the rule, but in many cases, the rule applies. It is not just the exceptions; instead, its "What Your Odds or Chances Are?" to become.

---

[9] WHAT BLACKS NEED IS ECONOMIC POWER-Daily Press. https://www.dailypress.com/news/dp-xpm-20081119-2008-11-19-0811180076-story.html

[10] https://www2.deloitte.com/content/dam/Deloitte/global/Documents/Energy-and-Resources/dttl-ER-Shipping-Tax-Guide-6countries.pdf

If a culture has no strong economic base, then it resembles a plantation, not a community. The civil rights movement was very much about gaining control over economic means, and not so much about [11]getting political power as an end in itself. Of course, the right to vote was a fundamental issue during the civil rights movement. Jobs were the reason Martin Luther King traveled to Memphis the week of his assassination. Civil rights are of little help if the individual cannot secure income and take advantage of the right to live and work where he pleases. Economic freedom is not decided by political parties or by social culture; it is determined by the individual willing to sacrifice all he has for all he desires.[12] *"As soon as sacrifice becomes a duty and necessity, there is no limit to the horizon, for what a man can accomplish (Ernest Renan). "*[13]

Who is The Thompson's?

THE MEETING OF MOTHER AND FATHER

There is a beginning to every man and woman's existence. Both of our parents were born in the early thirties and are native Floridians. Our mother is the older of three children; she was born in 1934, Cottondale, Florida (Jackson County). They lived in a rural area; farming was the main source of income. Our father is the second child of three children. He was born in Miami, Florida (Dade County); during that period, South Florida was both a vacation getaway and farming region. Our father was educated by the Broward County school system. Our mother completed high school in Panama City, Florida, because at the time, there was no senior high school in her hometown. After completing high school, our mother relocated to Hollywood, Florida, and stayed with her Aunt for a short time. Our mother and father met in Hallandale, Florida, where they wed and married on January 3, 1956. In their union, there were seven

---

[11] John S. Feinberg & Paul D. Feinberg, Abortion – Perfectio.... https://horvathliviu. wordpress.com/2011/03/14/john-s-feinberg-paul-d-feinberg-abortion/

[12] https://nationalcenter.org/ncppr/1997/01/01/too-much-political-power-not-enough-economic-independence/

[13] https://www.successories.com/iquote/author/1046/ernest-renan-quotes/1

children. One set of twins (Edward and Edwin), two other sons, and three daughters. Forty-four years ago, our parents were expecting their fourth child. Our mother was hospitalized because of complications with her pregnancy. Unfortunately, this pregnancy resulted in a miscarriage. She remained in the hospital for a short time to recover. My twin brother and I were two years old, and our younger brother was one year old at the time. *In route going home that day from the hospital, our father lost control of the car and plunged into the canal with all three siblings. That day God had taken one life but spared four others. It was God's will that we survived that ordeal.*

During our adolescent years, our mother was a homemaker and domestic worker. Our father was an auto-body repairman and coconut souvenirs maker. He learned to make souvenirs from his late grandfather, who was a native of the Bahamas, and later immigrated to South Florida in the late 1940s. In 1966, our mother started her paraprofessional career at Memorial Hospital, located in Hollywood, Florida. She worked there for about thirty years. Our official hometown is South Florida, and we move there in the summer of 1970. At the time, all the kids were in high school, and all graduated from the Broward County public school system. Six of the seven children are college graduates. The 1960s and the 1970s were a turbulent and uncertain time for the country and Black America. Segregation and discrimination were the norms during this period. We are a product of that period; I remember the events that brought our country to the brink of moral and social change. Supreme Court's decision upheld the Constitution of the United States and declared that all men are created equal. Protestors marched on Washington, D.C., and courthouses around the country used nonviolent techniques to fight for our inalienable rights and the right to vote.

Our creativity was inherited from our father and nurtured by observing and watching him make coconut souvenirs. Our father grew up in New York City, during his early adolescence, he always boasts about the City of New York and the world's fair (what the future will be like). Those stories, whether real or imaginary, influence our ability to "be a dreamer and try to turn those dreams into reality." Our father always said, *"In my father's house, there are many mansions if it were not so, I would have told you so."*

On the other hand, our mother always said, *"to understand the life you have to learn from your experiences." Maybe, experience is simply the name we give our mistakes (Oscar Wilde)[14]*. During this period, the Thompson family represented the character, size, and endured the daily hardship of a typical black family. Still, the next chapters depict the challenging experiences of two twins-Dreams, Hope, and Passion in seeking the American Dream.

2. Edward's

2.1. Experiences (Dreams. Hope & Passion)

EDWARD LATER ADOLESCENCE

If the question were posed-what would you change in life? Many people will say they would change something in there past or do things differently. I would not change anything that has to happen in my life. I am pleased with my past success and failures. Past reflections are incredibly helpful in establishing an understanding of the factors that shaped our life. My parents had seven children, four boys, and three girls. My twin brother and I were the first-born; I was born five minutes before him. The impact of a large family indirectly had a lasting effect on the way I preceded the size and function of a family structure. Before our parents moved to their present home, we live in a shotgun duplex apartment. At the evening meal, there were no leftovers at the kitchen table, what you did not eat someone else ate. During my early adolescence, the pastor of our church shapes my attitude toward what a man should be. He was short in stature but had a commanding voice when he spoke. He valued reading books and the importance of education. He believed that the man should manage household finance. From that statement, you may consider him to be a male chauvinist, but I believe what he was trying to convey, that control must be exercised with household finance. Poor household finances have destroyed many households and relationships.

---

[14] *https://www.brainyquote.com/quotes/oscar_wilde_105029*

High School

My first job was with the summer Youth Development Corporation; this was a turning point in my life. Both my twin brother and I were accepted into the program. A portion of my money was used to assist the family and the remaining for school clothing and other miscellaneous items. Coming from humble beginnings, you realize to get ahead in life; you must work. The second important job I obtain was working at the local laundry. My twin and I work in the soil department, where all the dirty laundry came in from customers (hospital, restaurants. hotel and other miscellaneous businesses, etc.).

My twin and I pooled our money together to buy our first car. This was a nineteen seventy-one Pontiac Lemans, two-door sedan, black exterior, and interior car with low mileage. During our junior and senior years, we were able to drive to school instead of riding the school bus. Of course, that elevated our social status among our peers. The only class that my brother and I attended together was our architectural drafting class.

In our junior year in high school, we both decided to go to Florida A&M University and majored in architecture engineering. Both of us were excited about being accepted to Florida A&M University. June of the following year, we graduated and were ready to attend college in the fall. After graduation, we both continued working at the local riverside laundry. Each milestone in our life, we received words of wisdom to keep our focus. One notable metaphor comes to mind it states, *"we dreamed, dreams because dreams are a part of reality, and reality is afoot-hole into the future" (The Thompson's Quote)*. During that period, I was listening to friends who graduated with us; they were talking about the Air Force (travel, training, and adventure). The recruiter told me that I would be able to fly. I discovered differently on active duty. Later I found out that the folks that get the flying opportunities were those who graduate from the Air Force and the Naval Academy.

Edward's Military Career Path

EDWARD'S U.S. AIR FORCE

When I began my Air Force career, our country was withdrawing troops from South Vietnam; the country was going through social and economic strife. The opposite was happening when I retired from active duty. [15]The Cold War between the United States and the Soviet Union was over. The United States had defeated its long-time adversary employing our economic and technological power. However, joining the Air Force changed my life for the next twenty years. I enlisted for six years and became an Airman First Class after basic training. I reported to basic training at Lackland Air Force Base, San Antonio Texas, on September 24, 1974. This was the first time in my life; my twin brother and I were separated. Now I was on my own, searching for my identity and future destiny in life. My twin brother was an extrovert, and I an introvert. In May 1975, after completion of initial technical training, I was assigned to RAF Chicksands England, United Kingdom.

A station in England was a cultural change. After completing the newcomer's briefing, I adjusted well. The first young lady I dated wanted to marry. Coming from a family of nine (father, mother, and seven children), marriage is a serious step at the time I was only eighteen years old. I was not ready for marriage. As the months went by, observing other airmen and associates who did marry English girls, there was a trend; they were only getting married to come to the United States. I realize they were great girlfriends but not good wives. A lot of positive things were accomplished in England: completed 18 semester hours at the University of Maryland, realize that this thin, tall, good-looking young man had charm. To enhance my image, I brought a red 1977 Triumph TR-7 sports car with sunroof top (always fascinated by cars) and shipped it back, after completion of my two-year tour of duty in Chicksands, England. I was approaching my 21st

---

[15] The Cold War between the United States and the Soviet.... https://www. dummies.com/education/history/american-history/the-cold-war-between-the-united-states-and-the-soviet-union/

birthday when I arrived back to the United States; "I was young, single with dreams and plenty of optimism." The next two years will be darkest and trying years of my life. My mother said, *"to understand the life you have to learn from your experiences."* She was right. I met a young lady several months after arriving at Langley, AFB, Virginia. She was from England, which was a surprise (attracted and well built). There was one thing wrong; she was married. When I told her that I did not date married women, it broke her heart. It was a true test of my moral development. I met another young lady shortly after; this is the time my life would be turned upside down. We got along great in the beginning (she was fun, exciting, full of life and adventure). From the surface, she portrayed herself as an honest, moral, and a person with integrity.

I learned several things from this experience. It applies to male or female; you must choose your spouse wisely. Everything should be taken into consideration their past, family values, morals, and what they want out of life. I develop the mental toughness that is required to conquer challenges and met adversities. Deep down in my heart, I knew I would marry again. Good things start occurring again after arriving at Homestead AFB, Florida, promoted to Staff Sergeant (E-5), which meant more money and started taking classes at Miami-Dade Community College. In February 1980, I met a beautiful young lady that captured my heart. I had an opportunity to meet her entire family (father, mother, and all six sisters); you could sense the love that the family had, something I did not feel in my first marriage. She was not materialistic but a fun-loving and exciting person to be around. My mother met her and love her (mother's approval is always a blessing); it was a match made in heaven.

I received an assignment to go to San Vito, Italy, reporting date March 1981, a month later received notification of a three-month advance training course at NTTC Corry Station, Pensacola, Florida, before going to Italy. This changed my reporting date to September 1981. I proposed to her after completion of advanced training in July of 1981. We set our wedding date for April 1982. Before leaving to go to Italy, I taken 45 days of leave. I did not have enough time to plan and get married before going to Italy, I asked, my fiancée to hold-on and be patience for my return, she agreed. I departed for Italy in September 1981; true love can withstand all challenges and endure separation. After completion of my certification training, I was able to return to the United States to get married.

For the second time in my Air Force career, I re-enlisted again for six years. My family and I had a wonderful time in Italy before leaving Italy my wife spoke more Italian than I. At this time, I was on active duty for eight years five duty assignments and traveled overseas twice. It was time for me to settle down and establish roots. I was selected for a special duty assignment as a technical training instructor at Pensacola Naval Air Station. Hello, Florida, here we come.

TRANSITION TO CIVILIAN LIFE

No matter what we pursue in life, your goal is to make sure that you have a plan. As always, there is an exception to every rule. (Plan or No Plan that is the Question) That is not always the case; the best of plans may fall short of its intended objective. Then, what is your next step? Quit, stay the course, or take another approach to reach your objective. There are difficulties and tough decisions that must be made when considering changing your plan. In other words, physiological and psychological obstacles; some seem or un-seem ones that would derail or change the course of events. The following are events and hurdles that I conquer to achieve my primary objective. A well-paid and secure job to fulfill my retirement investment goals.

My first objective was to obtain full-time employment. One of the things they cover in the transitional military program, the majority of jobs you will get would come from networking (people you know) and that what happened to me. My brother-in-law works for a major electric power provider in Florida; they were hiring temporary workers for heavy maintenance. At the time, the pay was more than the minimum wage. This opportunity was an eye-opening experience on what the civilian work environment was all about. Some workers enjoyed their job work and others complaining about it. Other temporary employees and I were wishing that we had the chance to be full-time instead of temporary employees. I knew before I separate from active duty that I need to be re-trained into the communications field. ATI Technical Training Center was my primary choice of training; the program was a well-rounded one, consisting of four major technical areas of study. I worked during the day and attended class during the evening; this continues for a year and a half. Approximately halfway through my program, an opportunity came about for a full-time position at a local copier and fax service company, my technical training instructor provide me with this employment lead. This was impeccable timing; my temporary job at the nuclear power plant was coming to an end.

Working as a service technician at the copier and fax service company was great. The experience and the intrinsic rewards repairing machines coupled with the gratitude from customers for a job well done. There was one drawback, a lot of work but little pay. I have a financial motto: *"to increase wealth, you must reduce expenses and increase income."* The income coming in was not enough to meet my living expenses; the only answer to my dilemma was to get another job. At this time, I was still attending ATI Technical Training Center, during one of my class breaks, I viewed the bulletin board, and there was a job listing for a part-time position working weekends at satellite communication company. This job was similar to the one I had in the Air Force. Now, I am working seven days a week and attending school. One-year pass by, my original company (copier and fax service) was brought by one of the fortune 500 companies. Things will get better now, more benefits, increase salary and bonuses. Those things did not happen; I learned one thing about this experience. A large company does not take good care of their people. The only individuals they are concerned about are their shareholders getting a return on their investment. Approximately two-years has passed, my hourly rate was at $8.50 per hour, and our original service manager and two senior field service technicians had departed the new company for greener pasture. One of the senior field service positions was posted, so I submitted my application and supported documentation for the job. Several weeks had passed by with no response on who was to fill the position. On a service call downtown, at a large law firm, one of the lawyers began using profanity at me when I arrived to service the copier, which was the last "straw" as a service technician with that company. Wednesday of that week, I called a salesperson I knew from the original company, he set-up and personal interview with the owner/service manager for possible employment with his company. The interview occurred that evening, It went well, and I was hired to begin on the following Monday (making one dollar more per hour). Not satisfy with my employment situation, I continue to search and keep my eyes open for a better opportunity.

My big opportunity came about, the senior satellite technician submitted his resignation and two week's notice, and there was now a full-time position open for me. I will never forget that Thursday night at approximately 10:00 p.m., I answer the phone, and the vice president of the company offer me a position as a technician full time, starting salary per year $31,500, medical and dental insurance paid by the company. Four years of doubting my ability, trying to maintain a positive attitude, my big break came, words cannot express the joy and excitement that came from a life's changing event. Six months later I was the operation's supervisor. One year later, site supervisor in charge of the entire operations, the company needs, and my personal needs were both satisfied. They had a dependable, reliable, and dedicated individual to oversee the operations, and I had the job and position that I strive for in the last four years.

There are a beginning and an end to everything in life. We all have to make decisions, whether it is right or wrong, good, or bad. The transition from military life to civilian life had all of the drama and excitement of a blockbuster movie with highs and lows, success, and failures. Despite all of the challenges, I overcame them all. I had to dig deep into my subconscious and tell myself you are a winner and the hardest working person around. The key to my success is a link to my perseverance, having a positive attitude.

High School Reunion 30 Years Later

The Class of 1974 Class Rolls Statistics:

625	Students
62	Black Students
15	Decease
53	Class Reunion Attendees

Only 2 (two) Black Students Attended the 30yr Class Reunion. Guest Who?

3. Edwin's

3.1. Experiences (Dreams. Hope & Passion)

OUR DREAMS

From the beginning of human man, in his striving effort to reach upward toward his creator, man has regarded dreams as genuine psychic phenomena. In some cases, dreams revolved around our work occupation, situations, and daily life circumstances. Most western religious leaders viewed dreams as communication with God, either for personal contact or a message for the congregation. Plato viewed dreams as a phenomenon for reaching into the inner spirit of man. He believed that dreams were communication between the inner and outer core of man. Whereas, the broader understanding of one's dream revealed that many have gradually realized the benefits and the aspects of their dreams as an enabler of life's aspirations. Modern psychologists have tended to limit their evaluations of dreams; however, the more progressive, experimental psychologists are beginning to realize that dreams are the key to life's aspirations. Generally, the twin's psychic might share a portion of dreams in terms of understanding its place as the foundation of life experiences. However, I believe my dreams as a kid has established the foundation for my life efforts and experiences. Childhood dreams often stay with us; they are echoes of our attitudes that underlined our thinking without us even realizing the impact.

My Role Models, Dream Facilitator, and Mentors

ROLE MODELS AND MENTORS

Childhood dreams and role models are nurturing components of child development. All role models can provide encouragement, positive reinforcement, and guidelines for success to any child that is in need. Although our society focuses on the individual and a person's success, our society must change to encompass the idea that "it takes a village to raise a child." Being a role model to a young person who is in desperate need of positive reinforcements will benefit our future society in ways easily imagined. Role models, whether they are educators, community members, or others, can be seen as welders melding their experience and education to reinforce life lessons in young people's lives.[16] In reflecting on my childhood of who were my role models, they consist of a variety of individuals in which I had personal contact, or I seem a variety of their deeds over time. In general, many of our role models are not named superstars or sports personalities, but they are fathers, mothers, aunts, teachers, and siblings. *Children are in need of role models and take them from all areas that are close at hand, whether mass media, parents, or their teachers."(Daniel Rose)* [17]

I never discounted our father as a good role model. But it was quite apparent as I got older. I did not want to be like my father. He had behaviors that were destructive to a productive life. On the other hand, he had some good traits. Our father did have a substance-abuse problem. When he was intoxicated, he was always trying to sing – "The Duke of Earl"; his middle name was "Earl" (See Appendix for Mentoring Details).

---

[16] https://serendipstudio.org/exchange/alesnick/extra-classroom-teachers-role-models

[17] Rose, D. (2004) 'The potential of role-model education, the encyclopedia of informal education, www.infed.org/biblio/role_model_education.htm.

The Lyrics for the Original Song:[18]

"As I walk through this world
Nothing can stop the duke of earl
And you, you are my girl
No one can hurt you, oh, no"

Dad's Version:
As I walk through God's World
Nothing can harm me because I am
The Duke of Earl

There was a significant difference in the lyrics.

We met our local pastor through some family friends known as the Magee's. Even though we never discounted our father as a role model, we also had other individuals who represented better role models; one such person was our local pastor. Our church was part of primitive Baptist association of independent black Baptist churches in the United States that were joined in a national convention in 1907. The custom-developed from black congregations formed after the Civil War by emancipated slaves who had previously attended Primitive Baptist churches with whites. Although they have followed much of the doctrine and practice of the white Primitive Baptists, the black Primitive Baptists set up a national convention and have established Sunday schools and aid societies, all of which are rejected by the whites. In the late 20th century, the convention had more than 250,000 members.

As you might imagine, there is always a need for spiritual growth and moral guidance. Having a spiritual component in our life at a young age allowed me to overcome that sense of hopelessness. Indeed, I can remember days of despair and hopelessness. Allowing a child to grow in their faith and giving them a strong foundation on which to build their lives, with a good understanding of life virtues, the reason for love and commitment is crucial. The timing of spiritual growth is equally

---

[18] https://www.last.fm/music/Gene+Chandler/_/Duke+of+Earl/+lyrics

important also. The real question should be posed; what is the best time for spiritual growth to occur? Should it occur in early childhood or at adulthood? Generally, there is an exception to every rule. Still, based on life experiences, a hypothesis can be drawn to whether a better understanding of spiritual growth and moral guidance is most beneficial at adulthood. Life experiences are the building blocks of that process. Consequently, if there are no life experiences, appreciation, and purpose is not meaningful. *"Life is the only real counselor; wisdom unfiltered through personal experience does not become a part of the moral tissue "(Edith Wharton).*[19] *Likewise," human beings, which are almost unique in having the ability to learn from the experience of others, are also remarkable for their apparent disinclination to do so "(Douglas Adams).*[20]

The other role model in our life was a local developer. He did tax-preparation; he was an insurance agent and also a local real estate developer. Some called him *"as a change-maker"* I never met him personally, but we heard so much about him and observed his business activity. It seems to be commonplace and especially if you are doing taxes, providing insurance, and buying and selling real estate that someone will notice your work and be infatuated about your successes.

He had a passion for creating change in previously neglected neighborhoods. He was a builder who uses old-fashioned hope and new affordable housing as weapons against blighted areas. It has been quite impressive 40 years later Edward and I were doing taxes and selling insurance and other financial services. In the early 80s, I purchased some properties, but that business activity never took off. The early 80s was the time of high inflation, and mortgage rates went as high as 13%.

---

[19] Edith Wharton-Life is the only real counselor; wisdom.... https://www.brainyquote.com/quotes/edith_wharton_131848

[20] Perennials forum: Winter hardy Alstroemeria-Garden.org. https://garden.org/thread/view/34190/Winter-hardy-Alstroemeria/

My Childhood Experience

MY EARLY CHILDHOOD & MIDDLE SCHOOL

I can remember several instances where we got a chance to see our grandmothers from both sides of the family. Later in life, I realized that both grandmother's name begins with the letter "I" (Izetta and Inez). In the 1960s, several hurricanes form in the Caribbean, and Inez was one of them. I can remember quite clearly a few storms, which hit South Florida in the early 1960s. Hurricane Donna battered south Florida and the entire U.S. East Coast in 1960. Donna's hurricane's eye passed 60 miles west of Miami, sparing Broward County. Unfortunately, residents in the Florida Keys fared worse, having to endure 13-foot storm surges and 150 mile-per-hour winds. Bridges were washed away, and homes resembled splintered matchsticks for miles. Hurricane Donna was the fifth-strongest hurricane of record to hit the U.S., causing 50 deaths, $387 million in property damage and affected over 50 million people according to the National Hurricane Center. [21]

While in middle school, Edward and I were always placed in separate classes. This occurred from elementary through middle school. I Learn how to play the flute, and Edward took typing. My junior high school band instructor graduated from Florida A &M University (FAMU), and he played in the FAMU Marching 100. Many of my junior high classmates played in the old high school marching band at the local School.

Hope

Whatever dreams we recall or merely imagine; basic human needs are essentially the same. How people go about meeting those needs, the obstacles, which they encounter in doing so, and the nature of their encounters with other individuals make up part of the complicated picture

---

[21] 1960-Hurricane Donna-South Florida Sun Sentinel.... https://www.sun-sentinel.com/news/sfl-1960-hurricane-story.html

of life. Understanding the nature of life challenges, and the rules and value judgments under which life is conducted should help most individuals cope with life more effectively. The coping process consists of hope. *"Hope is the thing with feathers That perches in the soul And sings the tune without the words And never stops at all."-Emily Dickinson* [22]

College

EDWIN'S COLLEGE DAYS

The summer of 1974 was the parting of the twins. Edward and I worked at the local laundry processing center that summer as if we had no care in the world. I had the opportunity to be a first-generation college-bound family member. Having time to reflect, this new endeavor presented challenges, which I never experience. At the time, there was no financial safety net available to support me if things went wrong. Edward had the U.S. Air Force, and I guess I had my extroverted personality and hope to rely on it. My next five years at Florida A & M University profoundly change my life. The happiness, the emotional roller coaster, the low points, and the financial despair will be with me for the rest of my life. This is where the Thompson's notable dream metaphor became a reality because of the next five years as part of life's existence, which neither my parents nor I had any clue on how to deal with these new challenges. "First Generation College Bound"

1974 Freshman Year

COLLEGE FRESHMAN YEAR

Florida A&M University is located in Tallahassee, Florida. Florida's Capital City has a unique history. Nestled among the hills, red clay, and oaks of Florida's panhandle, Tallahassee may not seem like the typical Florida city. Yet the history of Florida and Tallahassee are closely

---

[22] https://www.poemofquotes.com/emilydickinson/hopeisthethingwithfeathers.php

connected. "Tallahassee" is an Apalachee Indian word meaning "old town" or "abandoned fields." Tallahassee's tall hills attracted search parties in the early 1800s. In 1824 the City of Tallahassee was created, with a log cabin as the capital. Even today, the log cabin is still located on the capitol lawn. Founded in 1887, Florida A& M University was built on the highest of seven hills. For 90 years, Florida A& M University has served as a beacon of light in man's never-ending quest for equality and justice, shaping men and women from all walks of life into successful, responsible, and productive citizens. *"It is through this history of ambitions, abilities, and achievements, strive for and attained, that their students build dreams and hopes for the future"* (Source: Florida A&M – 1977 Yearbook).

As beginning freshmen, we all stayed on campus. I remained in Gibbs Hall. Gibbs Hall was constructed in 1955. It was named in honor of Thomas Gibbs. Mr. Gibbs introduced the bill to the Florida Legislature that provided for the establishment of a college.[23] Gibbs Hall is located in the West Quadrangle of campus on Wahnish Way directly across the street from the Bragg Memorial Stadium, and north of the "Patch," The Patch is where the FAMU Marching 100 practiced. FAMU's Marching 100 is known for its great marching, which consists of 200 steps per minute, incredible showmanship, and excellent musicianship. I had great respect for FAMU's music department because I was in the marching band when I was in high school. Even though I enjoyed playing in our high school marching band, I could not try out for the marching band and keep up with my engineering classes, so I cancel my Marching 100 band tryouts. I guess every man must know their limitation. It always seems that all freshmen become bored with on-campus life. So, after my freshman year, I decided to live off-campus, and the financial aid money was rolling end. I knew I needed some better living quarters than Gibb's Hall.

ENGINEERING MAJOR SELECTION

While in high school, I took architectural drafting for four years. So, when I graduated from high school and decided to attend FAMU, I was ready for

---

[23] http://www.famu.edu/Purchasing/UserFiles/File/presentation.pdf

all the Architectural Engineering classes. *In general, engineering comprises of any kind of activity, which aims at either solving a problem or completing a task related to a definition, design, specification of a product, service, or function.* Even though I started as an architectural engineering major, I changed my major to civil engineering in 1975. This change was brought about when I met Paul, who was a Vietnam vet. The other influence was that most architects only design the building, and after the building is built, there is no further need for the architect's services. However, with civil engineering projects, the road gets built, the road ages and has to be maintained, and consequently, over time, the roadway needs to be replaced. With that type of life cycle, I will always have a job and be in demand. That particular change in major set the stage for an outstanding engineering career, and I am incredibly grateful. That real change in major set me up for an internship with the City of Tallahassee at their wastewater treatment facility. After reflecting that experience obtained from that internship was the catalyst for my first professional job as an environmental engineer with the State of Michigan in 1979.

I was fortunate to be in the right place at the right time. A representative from the City of Tallahassee wastewater department needed a wastewater technician. My instructor informed me of the opportunity. I followed up and was soon hired under the Comprehensive Employment and Training Act of 1975 (CETA) program. The primary purpose of CETA was to provide job training and employment opportunities for economically disadvantaged, unemployed, and underemployed persons and to assure that training and other services lead to maximum employment opportunities. The other objective of the program was to enhance individual self-sufficiency by establishing a flexible and decentralized job training system for Federal, state, and local programs (Jimmy Carter Administration).

EDWIN'S ARMY ROTC & NATIONAL GUARD SERVICE

When I graduated from High school in 1974, I was anti-war. But Edward did sign-up for the U.S. Air Force. It is quite ironic over time I changed my mind and signed up for the Army Reserve Officers' Training Corps

(ROTC) in 1975.-Army ROTC as it exists today, began with the signing of the National Defense Act of 1916, by President Woodrow Wilson. Military training had been taking place at civilian colleges and universities as early as 1819. Still, the signing of the National Defense Act brought this training under a single, Federally controlled agency. [24]

College ROTC is the American military's largest officer generating organization, having commissioned more than a half-million-second lieutenants. The first group, 133, received their commissions during the school year from 1919-20. In the school year, 1969-70 more than 16,500-second lieutenants received their gold bars through the program. Women were first accepted into Army ROTC in 1972. The first group of females, 150, was commissioned in the school year 1975-76. Women traditionally constitute roughly 20 percent of the cadets, and more than 15 percent of the commission officer ranks.

Army ROTC is not a college major; rather, it is a series of elective courses taken in conjunction with a student's progress toward the baccalaureate degree. Cadets generally take class instruction for four years, plus a six-week summer camp. A student must be enrolled in college full-time for not less than two years to earn a commission. The process traditionally commissions 65 percent of the second lieutenants that join the active Army, the Army National Guard, and the U.S. Army Reserve. More than half the current active Army General Officers are products of the ROTC system. [25]

General. Colin Powell, former chairman of the Joint Chiefs of Staff, earned his commission through ROTC at the City University of New York. General George Decker (Lafayette College), Fred Weyand (University of California-Berkeley), and General Gordon Sullivan (Norwich University) are former Army chiefs of staff who received commissions through the Army ROTC. General of the Army George C. Marshall, Army chief of

---

[24] ROTC cadet becomes second lieutenant, engaged in one great.... https://www. army.mil/article/187559/rotc_cadet_becomes_second_lieutenant_engaged_in_ one_great_afternoon

[25] colonels' attalion Cadet Handbook. https://armyrotc.eku.edu/sites/armyrotc.eku. edu/files/files/CadetHandbook_Pocket_May2015b1.pdf

staff during World War II, is a graduate of a school (Virginia Military Institute), which is part of the ROTC program. For many, the 1970s was a decade of pessimism. It opened with a recession in 1970 and the painful ending of the Vietnam War. Memories of the Great Depression made policymakers unwilling to use restrictive monetary and fiscal policy to contain inflation because it was felt that the associated increase in unemployment would be unacceptable.1) Instead, wage and price controls were introduced in August 1971. 2) An oil embargo, in 1973, brought on by the Organization of the Petroleum Exporting Countries (OPEC), led to rapid inflation and a recession.[26] It seems to reason that my motivation for joining ROTC was pure economics.

In 1975 I started Army ROTC Summer Camp at Fort Knox, Kentucky. Fort Knox was the home of the U.S. Army Mechanized Infantry Cavalry. American soldiers occupied the Fort Knox area as early as the Civil War. In 1862 the 6th Michigan Infantry constructed fortifications and bridges north of the present reservation boundaries. Fort Duffield, overlooking the town of West Point, was the site of one of these positions. Both the Union and Confederate armies operated in this area during the war. Union troops from the commands of Gen. Don Carlos Buell and Gen. William Tecumseh Sherman occupied Louisville and the hills overlooking the Ohio River. The brilliant Confederate cavalry leader from Lexington, John Hunt Morgan, raided the area with the 2nd Kentucky Cavalry in 1862, capturing several hundred federal troops.[27]

Fort Knox Mechanized Force was first assembled at Fort Eustis, Va., in the fall of 1930. It was organized as a combined arms force, which included armored cars, truck-drawn artillery, engineers, anti-aircraft artillery, and infantry tanks. The tank company assigned to the force-Company A, 1st Tank Regiment is today Company A, 1st Battalion, 66th Armored Regiment. It is the oldest tank unit in the U.S. Army. The Mechanized Force: however, became too closely associated with cavalry operations, and in 1931, the War Department disbanded it. No reason seemed to exist to

---

[26] Compensation in the 1970s-Bureau of Labor Statistics. https://www.bls.gov/opub/mlr/cwc/compensation-in-the-1970s.pdf

[27] Fort Knox-Wikipedia. https://en.wikipedia.org/wiki/Fort_Knox,_Kentucky

maintain an organization whose mission appeared similar to that of an existing combat arm. Instead, in a new policy regarding mechanization, all combat arms were directed to develop their mechanized programs.[28]

The 1st Cavalry Mechanized Regiment was established in 1936 by the 13th Cavalry Regiment, which in turn traded its horses for tanks and, together with the 1st Cavalry, comprised the 7th Cavalry Mechanized Brigade. The pace of activity at Fort Knox picked up quickly in the late 1930s. In 1940 Fort Knox served as the center for cavalry mechanization and developed much of the tactics and doctrine, which the Armored Force currently used today.

1976-Summer Camp

In 1976 I attended Army ROTC Summer Camp at Fort Bragg, North Carolina. Fort Bragg is the U.S. Army's largest airborne facility with more than 45,000 military personnel. Widely known as the "Home of the Airborne and the Special Forces." Fort Bragg houses the 82nd Airborne Division, Special Operations Command, and the U.S. Army Parachute Team (the Golden Knights). Fort Bragg and neighboring Pope Air Force Base form one of the largest military complexes in the world. Fort Bragg is a rapid deployment post with a mission of being ready to fight anywhere in the world within 18 hours from notice of deployment. [29]

1978-Florida Army National Guard

In 1978 I joined the Florida Army National Guard. Shortly after joining Florida's Army National Guard, our infantry unit was scheduled for jungle training at Fort Sherman, Panama Canal Zone. Fort Sherman was home to The Jungle Operations Training Center (JOTC) consists of 23,000 acres

---

[28] Fort Knox, Kentucky-The Military Standard. http://www.themilitarystandard. com/army_base/ky/fort_knox.php

[29] Fort Bragg Reports Fifth Positive Coronavirus Case; Person.... https://wkml. com/2020/03/23/fort-bragg-reports-fifth-positive-coronavirus-case-person-is-cumberland-county-resident/

of single and double canopy jungle. Fort Sherman was surrounded on the North and Northwest by the Caribbean Sea, on the South and Southwest by the Rio Chagres and the East by Limon Bay and the Gatun Lake. The U.S. Army closed the JOTC operation in 1999 after the Canal Zone was turnover to Panama. Jungle Operations Training Center Inactivated April 1, 1999, Fort Sherman was handed over 30 Jun 1999 JOTC was the U.S. Army's training center for light infantry and special operations units from 1953 to 1999. and "keeping the Art of Jungle Warfare Alive.

After returning from National Guard training in the summer of 1978. My roommate accepted a manager's job in California. he and I rented a nice Victoria house with hardwood floors located on a corner lot. My previous roommate Curtis and I held numerous social gatherings at the Victoria big house. The fall of 1978 presented a variety of job opportunities. The last four years of college was coming to an end. I was going on my fifth year of school, and money was becoming very short. My CETA job was coming to an end, and I was looking for another part-time job. This effort was very exhausting because the economy in 1978 was in a recession, and Jimmy Carter was president.

However, the Fall of 1978 was a time for job recruiters to visit college campuses, and my previous roommate interviewed with a variety of companies one notable construction company was in Providence Rhode Island. He had a successful interview with Gilbane construction company, and I guess the best man won the interview process. I lost out and was very upset and desperate for a great job offer. I interviewed seven different potential companies and was fortunate to land site visits with three out of the seven likely companies. My interview choices consist of the following:

1. State of Michigan – Michigan Dept of Civil Service, Lansing Michigan
2. Gilbane Construction Company, Providence Rhode Island [30]
3. Southern Railways, Atlanta Georgia
4. State of Georgia-DOT, Atlanta Georgia
5. State of Illinois – DOT, Springfield Illinois

---

[30] https://www.gilbaneco.com/

6.   Shell Oil Company, Delaware
7.   Avco Lycoming, Stratford Connecticut

1979 Spring Job Offer and Departure to Michigan

TRYING TO LAND THAT FIRST PROFESSIONAL JOB

When things start to go wrong-it does not stop. Winter of 1979, my Monte Carlo got repossess, my CETA job ended, and cash flow was short again. Whatever scene we recall or merely imagine, basic human needs are essentially the same. How people go about meeting those needs, the obstacles which they encounter in doing so, and the nature of their encounters with other individuals make up part of life complicated picture. Understanding the nature of social conditions, how relationships are structured, and the rules and value judgments under which life is conducted should help an individual cope with life more effectively. When your money is funny, everything is screwed up. Whether money is the root of all evil is a matter of opinion. America is a "Market Economy." The "Have's and Have Nots."

The Spring of 1979. After spending five years at Florida A&M University, it was time to leave. My money was running out; my patience was at an all-time low. My roommates left for Tampa, Florida, and landed a construction management job in Providence, Rhode Island. I was waiting to land a job from one of the seven interview job opportunities, but I was coming up with goose eggs. April of 1979, I finally got a yes from the State of Michigan Department of Civil Service related to the on-campus recruitment selection for the environmental engineering position with the Michigan Department of Natural Resources, Division of Water Quality, Point Source Studies Section. It is quite intriguing to look back over 40 years and find out in the 60s and 70s our most considerable concern from an environmental standpoint was related to clean water, clean air, and proper disposal of waste in landfills. In the 60s and 70s, there was no talk about climate change. Fast forward to 2014, and we have the Flint water crisis.

The amazing thing about the Flint water crisis was the actual treatment process for groundwater was quite simple based on industry-standard treatment and distribution methods through iron and lead pipes. Drinking water treatment methods differ between regions, but in general, the treatment involves a few key steps consisting of aeration, flocculation, sedimentation, filtration, disinfection, and pipe leaching protection. Lead leaching from pipes into the water supply is a serious public health concern. And if water sources or treatment regimens are changed, the new chemistry can cause water distribution systems that were previously safe to begin releasing toxic lead. [31] This is "Basic Drinking Water Treatment 101". Need I say any more the drinking water treatment process is not moon-shot technology.

The winter and spring of 1979 was an "Invictus Moment"

Poem-Invictus [32]

Out of the night that covers me,
Black as the Pit from pole to pole,
I thank whatever gods maybe
For my unconquerable soul.
In the fell clutch of circumstance
I have not winced nor cried aloud.
Under the bludgeoning of chance
My head is bloody but unbowed.

Beyond this place of wrath and tears
Looms but the Horror of the shade,
And yet the menace of the years
Finds, and shall find, me unafraid.

It matters not how strait the gate,
How charged with punishments the scroll.

---

[31] Making lead pipes safe. https://phys.org/news/2019-04-pipes-safe.html

[32] William Ernest Henley-Out Of The Night That Covers Me. https://www.wussu.com/poems/wehootn.htm

I am the master of my fate:
I am the captain of my soul.
by William Ernest Henley

My Passion

EDWIN'S PROFESSIONAL CAREER PATH

Over the years, I have been involved in a variety of personal, business, and political activities. *These outside interests have broadened my horizons, and I have had the opportunity to see many of my childhood dreams come true.* While growing up in Southern Florida, our family lived close to Fort Lauderdale International Airport. Airports have always interested me. When I graduated from high school, my twin brother went into the Air Force. It was apparent that flying was our interest. Before graduating from college, the opportunity presented itself again. The U.S. Air Force in 1978 was looking for technical college grads to fill officer positions. I declined the offer because they could not guarantee me flight-training status. If I could not fly, I was not going to enlist.

In 1983, I received a promotion to work at the Michigan Department of Transportation Bureau of Aeronautics. The Bureau of Aeronautics was responsible for the planning, designing, and construction of airports. In 1987, I received my private pilot's license. Since childhood, I realized the value of following your interest and passion. *If you – believe it, dream it, you can make it become a reality.* The first half of my professional career was with the state of Michigan. In 1995 this was a deciding moment in my career. My airport development job was one of the best jobs I had since I became an engineer. My only request to my division administrator was that I would be willing to continue to do my current work function and have the opportunity to do some airport construction management work for the summer construction season. In many cases, if you had a conscientious and motivated employee, this request would be a no brainer. As in many organizations have problems in accommodating motivated employees. I guess that year. I had a flashback to 1979 when the Air Force offers me an opportunity to be a commission officer. My request was if you can guarantee me flight time, I will be willing to take up the offer. No flight time – No officer rank as Base Engineer. Flying was my passion.

There is a saying, "It's Better to Be Lucky Than Good." In 1995, I found my self in this same situation. Between 1990 to 1995 I ran for public office four-times unsuccessful. I got my name out in public and had the opportunity to see what potential politicians do to run for office. A gentleman by the name of Rodney informs me that General Motors Corporation was looking for potential candidates that might be interested in joining the organization as a production supervisor at Lansing Car Assembly. The neat thing about this opportunity was that GM had a production supervisory program. This program was a 12-month training program in all phases of the car production process. The production process consists of four major manufacturing areas:" Body, Paint, Trim, and General Assembly. Over the years, GM was protected of its engineering ranks. Typically, engineering talent came out of their GM-Kettering University[33]. Many of the GM young recruits are interns. The talent and skill hiring approach GM used was unique. The skill assessment process consists of an office in-basket test, employee exercises, role-playing, job simulation, videotaping, and your formal in-person interview.

After I look back on the job move, that was a bold move for me, leaving a perfectly valid state job working with airports, flying around in state aircraft, and operating as a pilot in command, and that dream job came to an end. Now I was heading to GM to supervise hourly workers on the production line. I spent a year and a half in production and got an opportunity to get back in the engineering ranks. That construction experience I sort after at the State of Michigan – I finally got my wish to work around production tooling, plant infrastructure, demolition of six old plants, and building two new production facilities in the Lansing Area. The 2008 Global Financial Crisis cause some exciting things to happen at GM. The thought of bankruptcy at GM what's an unthinkable episode, but it did happen, and I got caught right in the middle of layoffs and furloughs, a retirement offer was presented in 2009, and I took it like a scared rabbit, and I never look back. This was one in a lifetime moment for me at age

---

[33] https://www.kettering.edu/

53, a full retirement package, a full-service tax, and investment business along with insurance adjusting services. I was ready to roll the dice. Hello, Retirement Freedom.

The Entrepreneurial Experience

EDM Tax Service[34] started in 1984, providing basic tax preparation services. Since 1984 the entire tax preparation and financial services industry have changed. In 2006, EDM Tax Service launched its new financial service retail concept, better known as "TFS-Financial Store"[35] (TFS-01). This concept was marketed as a business opportunity/ franchise package. TFS-02 was located in South Florida in a professional office setting, and was anticipated after one year, it will be relocated to a retail outlet. Proposed service offerings were to consist of: Basic Tax Preparation, Full Investment, and Retirement Planning, Mortgages, non-profit development, and Insurance Adjusting Services.

4. The Children of Israel

4.1. The Span of Time:

There has never been enough time. Each human being has the same number of hours and minutes every day. Rich people cannot buy more hours. Scientists cannot invent new minutes. And you cannot save time to spend it on another day. Even so, time is amazingly fair and forgiving. *"No matter how much time you've wasted in the past, you still have an entire tomorrow."-Denis Waitley*[23]

---

[34] EDM Tax Services is owned & operated by the Co-Author Edwin E. Thompson, RIA, MBA

[35] https://sites.google.com/tfs-financialstore.com/tfs-financial-store/home ;owned & operated by the Co-Author Edwin E. Thompson, RIA, MBA

4.2. The Children of Israel Comparison

When making the comparison between the Children of Israel and Black Americans' struggle, the period between both groups of bondage and freedom covers four-hundred years. The first 200 years of the Children of Israel were in the land of Canaan, and the second two hundred years they were in the land of Egypt. And there were forty years that the Israelites spent in the wilderness. It was apparent that when the Children of Israel were in Egypt that they were in bondage by Pharaoh. Hence there was no time for the children of Israel to become productive individuals since they did not have control of their destiny. But when the opportunity presented itself, they still did not follow God's instructions and continued destructive behavior.

4.3. How long is A generation

Generally, the length of a generation roughly matches the time between birth and full adulthood. In America, a generation has ranged in length from 18 to 30 years. This 30-year span is more reflective of a time frame for our discussions. The span of an era during the Children of Israel was much longer than 30 years. This time could have possibly changed over time because Moses was reported to have lived beyond 125 years of age. Consequently, their generation timeline could cover between 50 to 100 years.

4.4. Why are Generations So Important in History?

It is vital because the self-correcting dynamic of generational action and reaction is precisely what gives modern history its cyclical rhythm. The linkage between generations and history runs in both directions. It is a generational change, for example, that offers modern history a transition between eras of political upheaval and periods of value upheaval. And it is the historical change between protective and permissive child nurture that plays a significant role in shaping a new generation differently from the last.

4.5. How Long Does it take to Establish a Productive Generation?

The time frame required to establish a productive generation. It is inversely related to the time needed to educate a productive generation. Based on father time, we all get 24 hours a day and 365 days a year with no repeats. The time is used and cannot be recycled. Generally, time should be used as wisely as possible. The Rockefeller family would be a benchmark in gauging the time required to establish a productive generation. It estimated that the Rockefeller family tree spans seven generations (7 x 30 = 120 Years). A majority of John D's. Wealth was acquired through oil holdings (See Appendix – Family Reunion Planner).

5. Taking Personal Responsibility

With freedom comes responsibility; to take responsibility for your life, is to take responsibility for your powers of thinking, feeling, speaking, and actions, because this is the structure of all *human experience*. You mainly support life experiences through your everyday actions. You take the actions you take. What this means is that nobody can make you think, feel, say, or do anything. *"Man must cease attributing his problems to his environment and learn again to exercise his will – his personal responsibility."*-<u>Albert Einstein</u>, [36]*"A sign of wisdom and maturity is when you come to terms with the realization that your decisions cause your rewards and consequences. You are responsible for your life, and your ultimate success depends on the choices you make."*-<u>Denis Waitley</u> [37]

We often use the Serenity Prayer as guidance for fostering the Duty of Responsibility.

---

[36] https://www.powerquotations.com/quote/man-must-cease-attributing-his-1

[37] When You Take Control Of Your Life, You Move Closer To …. https://medium.com/the-mission/when-you-take-control-of-your-life-you-move-closer-to-fulfilling-your-destiny-264d7d680d28

Serenity Prayer

God, grant me the serenity to accept the things I cannot change, Courage to change the things I can, and wisdom to know the difference. Father give us courage to change what must be altered, serenity to accept what cannot be helped, and the insight to know the one from the other, By Reinhold Niebuhr.[38]

9 Ways to Take Personal Responsibility for Your Life

1. Take Responsibility for your Thoughts, Feelings, Words, and Actions. [39]
2. Stop Blaming White People for our Problems. Evaluate whether it is a Systematic System Problem or a Cultural Problem.
3. Stop Complaining. Generally, people do not want to listen to your complaints. If you do not have anything positive to say, do not say anything at all.
4. Refusing to take everything Personal. Develop a thick skin.
5. Foster Happiness.
6. Live in the Present Moment.
7. Use the Power of Purpose.
8. Feel Calm and Confident.
9. Looking for the Good in People.

6. What Does it Take for Us to Believe in Each Other?

6.1. Why Don't we believe in each other?

Why don't we believe in each other? When we were in middle school, our local pastor told this story: "The saying, the white man's ice is colder?" I laughed and said no, but it sure seems like it. I said that because, to me, it seems more natural for white people to get ahead in this world. He said that "if they had to buy Uncle John's Ice versus the white man selling ice, black

---

[38] Serenity Prayer-Wikipedia. https://en.wikipedia.org/wiki/Serenity_Prayer

[39] 9 Ways to Take Responsibility for Your Life | Dina Marais https://dinamarais.com/2018/01/30/9-ways-to-take-responsibility-for-your-life/

people would buy the white man's ice." I asked him why, he responded, and he said, "The stupid fools use to think, THE WHITE MAN'S ICE WAS COLDER." As time went on, I learn in my chemistry class that water freeze at 32 degrees Fahrenheit so the white man ice can not be colder than Uncle John's Ice.

Even history books can confirm how long African-Americans have competed with one another. Divided by skin complexion as house and field Negroes, we were forced to create segregation within our race. Trickling down from generation to generation, African-Americans seem to embody still this desire to compete and tear one another down. [40]

Generally, Mexican, and Chinese cultures will come over to the United States and perfect their crafts just to return to their homes and give back. They continuously support their people in any endeavor they attempt to pursue. Unlike other races, many Mexican and Chinese are proud of their people no matter their socio-economic status or difference in skin complexion. We can be very much so envious while secretly wishing failure on each other. No matter if it is in the classroom or the corporate world, there seems to be a hesitation in African-Americans supporting one another. [41]

Black businesses can never fully succeed without the help of African-Americans. It begins with us first. Once we start to support one another, maybe we will start to see more Oprah Winfrey's and Cathy Hughes'. For even more African-Americans to succeed, African-Americans must support each other.

Most African-Americans are not impoverished. Almost half of the blacks surveyed in a Gallup poll supposed that three out of four African-Americans live in inner cities. Yet in 2001, most African-Americans are

---

[40] Why Black People Don't Support Each Other: Race....https://rnbphilly.com/2607255/
why-black-people-dont-support-each-other/

[41] Why Black People Don't Support Each Other: Race .... https://rnbphilly.
com/2607255/why-black-people-dont-support-each-other/

neither poor nor even close to it: by any estimation, middle-class blacks outnumber poor ones.

African-Americans earn 61 percent of what whites do. Though accurate as a nationwide median in 1995, this figure is dragged down by the disproportionate number of single black welfare mothers. Black two-parent families earned 87 percent of what white two-parent families made in 1995. Also distorting the median is the disproportionate number of blacks who live in the South, where wages are lower overall. If you look only at specific areas rather than at the nation, black household earnings in 1994 exceeded whites' in 130 cities and counties across the country. [42]

In the grip of this seductive ideology, blacks have made the immobilizing assumption that individual initiative can lead only to failure, with only a few exceptionally gifted or lucky exceptions. Yet many groups have triumphed over similar (or worse) obstacles—including millions of the Caribbean and African immigrants in America, from Colin Powell to the thousands of Caribbean children succeeding in precisely the crumbling schools where black American kids fail. Indeed, thinkers such as Thomas Sowell and Stephan and Abigail Thernstrom argue that American blacks could have advanced—and were advancing—even without the civil rights legislation of the sixties and the racial preferences of the seventies, since black unemployment was at an all-time low in the mid-sixties, and the black middle class was already growing fast. [43]

Blacks are not the only people who have sabotaged themselves through victimology. Take the eerily similar case of the Boston Irish, the target of contempt and discrimination in nineteenth-century America. By the 1920s, when anti-Irish bigotry had significantly receded, historical memory allowed Mayor James Michael Curley to maintain power by stoking Irish resentment very like today's black resentment. Curley found "anti-Irish" sentiment everywhere: merit hiring systems were "anti-Irish";

---

[42] https://www.city-journal.org/html/what%E2%80%99s-holding-blacks-back-12025.html

[43] What's Holding Blacks Back? | Articles About African Americans. https://www.city-journal.org/html/what%E2%80%99s-holding-blacks-back-12025.html

"Anglo-Saxon" culture was fatally diseased. Even today, the remnant of this mentality still traps members of South Boston's Irish community in crummy housing projects full of idle adults who have high rates of substance abuse. [44]

6.2. Refocusing Our Thought Process

It is our thought process; the way you think and your thought process of being able to associate and simulate events and circumstances around you. Black people have too much of an emotional attachment to everything, culturally, visually, and religiously. No left Brain-all right-brain visual inspiration as kids. With no role models, many kids are at a loss. My mother did not know what engineers do, and she did not know any engineers personally. So, when I studied and became an engineer, she did not show any excitement about my accomplishments. I did not take it personally. You can only associate and simulate events and circumstances that you are aware of.

7. What are my Odds of becoming?

In the 1960s, we listen to Walter Cronkite CBS Series "The 21st Century" he always talked about what it would be like in the 21st Century, where its flying cars or some modern invention. Most kids get the question of what they would like to be or what they would like to become when they grow up. In the '60s and '70s, I have always been intrigued about what we want to do when we grow up. And today, in this 21st Century, generally most kids are fascinated about what they would like to be when they grow up or what they want to be; a movie star, rapper, doctor, lawyer, professional athlete, president of the United States or Indian chief. *The twin's philosophy could be anything if you had enough time and money.*

---

[44] What's Holding Blacks Back? | Articles About African Americans. https://www.city-journal.org/html/what%E2%80%99s-holding-blacks-back-12025.html

Art Young, director of Urban Youth Sports at Northeastern University's Center for the Study of Sports in Society, came up with some staggering figures concerning the possibility of realizing a dream to become a pro athlete. Based on some extensive studies, he says that only 1 out of every 50,000 high school athletes will ever become a part of a professional team. To put those astronomical odds in perspective, that is like filling each seat at Denver's Coors Field (the home of the Colorado Rockies), then placing each name in a huge barrel. If yours is not the one, single name drawn, then—just like that—your lifelong dream is dead! [45]

Amazingly, even with those vast odds, Taylor (also education director for the award-winning movie, Hoop Dreams) says 66 percent of 7th-and 8th-grade African-American boys still firmly believe they can make a living in pro sports. That's 2 out of 3 youngsters who ignore these odds and continue the pursuit even though they clearly would be better served if the incredible determination, dedication, and time to prepare that's necessary to become an athlete were directed in areas where the odds to achieve are much less. And the odds are the following:[46]

Odds of a Person being Illiterate-1 in 10
Odds of owing a Small Business 1 in 1,000
Odds of becoming an Engineer 1 in 50,000
Odds of becoming a Doctor 1 in 100,000
Odds of becoming a Movie Star 1 in 110,500
Odds of Inheriting a $1 Million is 1 in 12 million
Odds of a person becoming an NBA Star – 1 in 10 million
Odds of a person becoming a Rap Star is 1 in 10 Million
Odds of becoming President of The United States: 1 in 10 million
Odds of being struck by lighting 1 in 23 million
Odds of winning the Florida Lotto 1 in 23 million

---

[45] The Post Hip-Hop Generation. https://posthip-hopgeneration.blogspot.com/
[46] Schacht Faces Retiree Wrath | Light Reading. https://www.lightreading.com/ ethernet-ip/schacht-faces-retiree-wrath/d/d-id/595723

7.1. The 10,000 Hours Rule 47

If the odds are in your favor, studies have suggested that it takes an average of 10,000 hours of practice to become an expert or master in a field. [48] The 10,000-hour rule is inspiring because it gives a figure, a statistic, a number to something authentic. A change occurs. A shift that you can see in almost anyone who reaches that point. You can see it in the sciences where Einstein has his 20,000 hours moment with the 2nd Theory of Relativity; you can see it in business in Edison and Tesla. [49] It is not just some wacky spiritual, occult concept. And it is sturdy, and everyone who is ever done anything important will explain, "I've had that feeling." It is intuition. Steve Jobs talks about it, and Einstein discusses it. Nobody else has written about it–Malcolm Gladwell and others spoke about that 10,000-hour rule for mastering a skill or interest. Ten thousand hours is approximately 417 days. If you devote 3 hours per day, it would be around 3333 days or nine-plus years. [50] "No Effort, No Pain, and No Gain," it is just that simple.

8. Our World

The World over time and social organization that began around 1820 in Great Britain and later in other countries, replaced hand tools with power-driven machines such as the cotton loom and the steam engine, with the concentration of industrial production in large establishments better known as the Industrial Age. In 1920, there were three essential things in life; they consisted of the following: "Food, Shelter, and Fire." In 2020, one

---

[47] https://www.quora.com/It-is-said-you-need-10-000-hours-to-master-a-skill-If-you-spend-3-hours-a-day-acquiring-a-skill-how-many-days-does-it-take-to-spend-10-000-hours-at-it

[48] "Mastering Creativity." Campaign, Haymarket Business Publications Ltd., Feb. 2015, p. 24.

[49] Outside the Lines With Rap Genius – OTL 61: Robert Greene …. https://genius.com/Outside-the-lines-with-rap-genius-otl-61-robert-greene-excerpt-2-the-10000-hour-rule-lyrics

[50] https://www.quora.com/It-is-said-you-need-10-000-hours-to-master-a-skill-If-you-spend-3-hours-a-day-acquiring-a-skill-how-many-days-does-it-take-to-spend-10-000-hours-at-it

hundred years later, there are still three essential things in life; they are: "Food, Shelter, and Energy." One hundred years from now, there would always be the need for: "Food, Shelter and Energy." It is believed that the Information Age supplanted the Industrial Age in the late 20th Century, a view that has become common since 1989. Many third world economies today have a manufacturing base. It is debatable whether civilization has left the Industrial Age or is still in it. Out of the Industrial Revolution came improvements in the standard of living and industrial production methods.

The Knowledge Model of the Information Age brought about-"The Internet" Between Google, Facebook, YouTube, and Twitter, there are questions of what the real truth on these information platforms is. There is a distinct difference between Information, Judgment, and Wisdom. Information is associated with data, as data represents values attributed to parameters, and information is data in context and associated with meaning attached to it. However, judgment is an opinion that you form, especially after thinking carefully. It also refers to the ability to make sensible decisions about what to do and when to do it. The fundamental piece of wisdom is the understanding of reality as it relates to living a good life; reasonable and practical, focusing on the real circumstances and character of each individual; good judgment about complex situations involving reflection, insight, and a plausible conception of the human spirit. Generally, wisdom comes with age, and some have genius ability insights." The Information Age (Internet) has generated a discussion on what real or fake. Information is Power; this is particularly important in seeking the American Dream in a Market-Driven Economy (See Appendix for The Knowledge Model).

8.1. A Market-Driven Economy

A market economy is a system where the laws of supply and demand direct the production of goods and services. Supply includes natural resources, capital, and labor. Demand includes purchases by consumers, businesses, and the government. [51] While a market economy has many advantages, such as fostering innovation, variety, and individual choice, it also has disadvantages, such as a tendency for an inequitable distribution of wealth and income for the general consumer. [52]The US consumer spending represents 65 to 70 percent of GDP buying power in the US economy. This is the underlying reason to create and maintain jobs to support the American consumer. "No Consumer-No Economy."

Can the last "50 years of Economic Activity" be duplicated? The answer is probably not for this reason. For many Americans in the working class and the middle class, upward mobility has served as the heart and soul of the American Dream, the prospect of "betterment" and to "improve one's wealth" for oneself and one's children. The approach was to "Work Hard, Save, and Send your kids to college so they can do better than you did, and retire happy with a Defined Benefit Pension, 457 Plan (Insurance Contracts), and 401K Plan, and move to a warmer climate" this has been the script for the last 50 years. For some American's, this approach has worked. While these studies point to where retirees may be likely to move, it is worth noting that most people end up staying in one place when they retire. Only 1.6% of retirees between the ages of 55 and 65 moved across state lines. Your circumstances at birth—mainly, what your parents do for a living—are an even more significant factor in how far you get in life than we had previously realized. [53] On the other hand, if you are first-generation educated like the Thompson twins, it is your Dreams, Hope, and Passion that makes the difference. In either case, you are the foundation for the next generation's success. The process only works if you have a flourishing economy at best. A recession or depression do not generate American Dream success.

There is a need for the US Market-Driven Economy to continue to flourish. The capital markets for the last 50 years have reflected the ups

---

[51] What goods and services should be produced in a market.... https://answersdrive.com/ what-goods-and-services-should-be-produced-in-a-market-economy-1740039

[52] 2. What are some of the advantages and disadvantages to a.... https://brainly.com/ question/5125346

[53] American Dream-Wikipedia. https://en.wikipedia.org/wiki/American_Dream The American Dream Scorecard-The Ford Foundation-Chasing The Dream (PBS)

and downs of the business cycle. A case can be made – that the capitalist system has worked too well. In the 1990s, efforts were undertaken to outsource information services and production output. The Chinese became a member of the World Trade Organization in 2001, Since 2001, a significant amount of US production output has been loss to the Chinese, but capital markets continue to reach higher values. Outside of the US, there are only five major population regions in the world that have promise for increased production and consumption growth. They consist of Russia, Brazil, India, China, and the African Continent.

9. Eight Principles of Personal Success

This is the list of the Twin's Eight Principle of Success:

1. Faith in God
2. Have a Dream
3. Think Positive
4. Take Personal Responsibility for your Actions
5. Working Well with Others
6. Using your God-Given Talent to Solve problems:
7. Study to show thyself approved unto God, a workman that needeth not to be ashamed, rightly dividing the word of truth (2 Timothy 2:15 King James Version (KJV). [54]
8. Have a Passion and/or a Personal Development Plan (PDP)
9. Maintaining Good Health

---

[54] Heritage Trail Bible Church. http://heritagetrailbiblechurch.org/

10. APPENDIX

The American Dream Scorecard – The Ford Foundation-Chasing The Dream (PBS) [55]

Several factors that shape how the twins think about the "American Dream" is our experiences. After all, who could better understand the challenges involved in moving up the socio-economic ladder than the twins on two different paths. Those who managed to navigate through the system, despite conventional wisdom. The Thompson Twins are real-life examples of what it takes to overcome life hardships and focus on the objective at hand. Reflection of the twin's experiences may serve as a template for others. We believe the journey is more process than related to pure luck. Our childhood dreams establish a mental foundation. Our hope and faith-not to give up or give in regardless of life circumstances and the passion for applying the 10,000 Hour rule to our work effort or interest. The PBS American Dream Scorecard asks respondents to answer 13 questions about their life. Each question represents a factor that research shows correlate to social mobility and happiness in life. Similarly, all the options within each question are also based on specific research related to mobility or positive life outcomes. Once completed, you receive a composite score and a list of factors working for and against you. The higher your score, the more you had to overcome. The lower the score, the more you had done in your favour. [56]

---

[55] https://www.fordfoundation.org/ideas/ford-forum/your-american-dream-score/

[56] How'd You Get Here? – Chasing the Dream. https://www.pbs.org/wnet/chasing-the-dream/stories/howd-you-get-here/

[57] How'd You Get Here? – Chasing the Dream. https://www.pbs.org/wnet/chasing-the-dream/stories/howd-you-get-here/

	The More You had working in your favor. [57]	The More You had to Overcome.
Score Taker	**Lower Score 50 or Less**	**Higher Score 51 or Greater**
1. Edwin		**63 out of 100**
2. Edward		**63 out of 100**
3.		
4.		

Chart By Co-Author Edwin E. Thompson, RIA, MBA 58

Check Others American Dream Score 3. & 4

Website Link: https://www.pbs.org/wnet/chasing-the-dream/your-american-dream-score/

---

[58] This Chart – Design by Co-Author – Edwin E. Thompson, RIA, MBA

MENTORING CHECKLIST

Three Types Of Mentoring.[59]

1. Traditional One-on-one Mentoring. A mentee and mentor are matched, either through a program or on their own.
2. Distance Mentoring. A mentoring relationship in which the two parties (or group) are in different locations.
3. Group Mentoring. A single mentor is matched with a cohort of mentees.

The Three C's of Mentorship

- Role 1: Consultant. This is the most prominent role for a mentor to play....
- Role 2: Counselor. Listen....
- Role 3: Cheerleader. In addition to all of the constructive feedback and advice that a mentor can give, they should also provide support and enthusiasm.

Seven Key Qualities That Can Help You Become An Effective Mentor.[60]

- Ability and willingness to communicate what you know.
- Preparedness.

---

[59] Assignment: Mentoring Unit – NursingPaperSlayers. **https://nursingpaperslayers.com/assignment-mentoring-unit/**

[60] What qualities have a good friend? | AnswersDrive. https://answersdrive.com/what-qualities-have-a-good-friend-2437785

- Approachability, availability, and the ability to listen.
- Honesty with diplomacy
- Inquisitiveness....
- Objectivity and fairness....
- Compassion and genuineness.

A Good Mentor Possesses The Following Qualities:[61]

- Willingness to share skills, knowledge, and expertise.
- Demonstrates a positive attitude and acts as a positive role model.
- Takes a personal interest in the mentoring relationship.
- Exhibits enthusiasm in the field.

---

[61] IT@Cornell Mentoring Program | IT@Cornell. https://it.cornell.edu/it-career-framework-itconnects/itcornell-mentoring-program

DREAMS, HOPE, AND PASSION

Eight Reasons That Children Dream of becoming a teacher is likely because school is defining childhood experience.

Childhood Dream Jobs:

When I Grow Up, I Want to Be:[62]

1. Teacher
2. Veterinarian
3. Doctor or Nurse
4. Professional Athlete
5. Ballerina
6. Police Officer
7. Firefighter
8. Pilot

Top 4 Jobs Which Require You To Work with Your Hands

Perhaps it is not surprising that carpentry has a bright future. Electrician. Similar to the increased demand in carpenters, welders, and Pipefitters for industrial and commercial projects are an integral part of new and existing construction projects (Vocational Education).

---

[62] Best, Bonitta. "Gospel Rookie Hits No. 1 on Billboard." The Triangle Tribune, vol. 17, no. 9, Charlotte Post Publishing Co., 10 May 2015, p. 6B.

1. Carpenter.
2. Electrician.
3. Welder.
4. Plumber/Pipefitter

How to Find Your Passion and Live a Fulfilling Life

1. Ask Yourself: Is There Something You Already Love Doing?
2. Find out What You Spend Hours Reading and Learning About.
3. Brainstorm.
4. Ask Around, and Surf for Possibilities.
5. Do not Quit Your Job Just Yet.
6. Give It a Try First.
7. Do as Much Research as Possible.
8. Practice, and Practice, and Practice Some More (Appy the 10,000 + Hour Rule).

THE KNOWLEDGE MODEL[63]		
INFORMATION JUDGMENT WISDOM		
INFORMATION	The Internet	
	Data Sources	Data Collection Methods	Tabulated Sources
	Ability To Make Sensible Decisions		
Judgment			
	Experience	Data Collection Tabulations	Empirical Observation
	Wisdom Comes With Age		
WISDOM			
	Based on Judgement	Empirical Observation	Applied Experience Over Time
			Data Types
			Data Collection
			Tabulated Sources
Knowledge: Is generally Associated with Facts, Truths, and Principles		
First Principles: The Building Blocks of True Knowledge		

---

[63] The Knowledge Model – TFS Modeling Methodology-by Edwin E. Thompson, RIA, MBA

REFOCUSING THE DREAM FAMILY REUNION PLANNER[64]

(The Family Tree-The Next Generation)

1. Recruit A Planning Committee

2. Scheduled Committee Meetings

3. Assign Responsibilities (such as attendance, finance, communication, venue, food, activities, etc.)

4. Set A Date And Place (survey relatives if need be)

5. Gather Relatives' Contact Information Or Update Contact List

6. Collect Starter Money (if a first-time reunion) or evaluate balance from the last reunion

---

[64] Your Family Reunion Planning Checklist. https://www.familytreemagazine.com/premium/family-reunion-planning-checklist/

<u>NOTES</u>

<u>NOTES</u>

<u>NOTES</u>

<u>NOTES</u>

11. BIBLIOGRAPHY

1 Archibald MacLeish. (n.d.). Retrieved 4 13, 2020, from Poetry Foundation: http://www.poetryfoundation.org/bio/archibald-macleish

Robinson, Morgan. "Thirst For The American Dream: The Lost City Of Flint 1." Michigan Sociological Review, vol. 32, Michigan Sociological Association, Oct. 2018, p. 170.

Rose, D. (2004) 'The potential of role-model education, the encyclopedia of informal education, www.infed.org/biblio/role_model_education.htm. Rose, Daniel. The Potential of Role-Model Education. Infed. 22 March 2005

Statistics, N. C. (2008). *National Center for Education Statistics (NCES) Home Page, part of the U.S. Department of Education*. Retrieved 4 13, 2020, from U.S. Department of Education: http://nces.ed.gov

12. ABOUT THE AUTHOR

The Thompson Twins are the oldest siblings out of seven kids. They were born and raised in South Florida, attended Hollywood Hills High School. Both parties' professional career span of over 30 years. Both twins held various financial services and insurance adjusting credentials. Edward graduated from Liberty University, and Edwin graduated from Florida A&M University and has an MBA from the University of Phoenix. Both twins possess strong technical credentials. Edward's technical expertise is in satellite communication. Edwin is a train and practicing engineer by profession. Edward is a retired Master Sergeant from the United States Air Force. Edwin is a retired engineer from General Motors Corporation

The twins are actively manufacturing and marketing alternative energy systems. In 2012, the twins imparted on prototype testing of Lithium-Ion battery packs for solar and wind systems. We have installed systems in over 25 states and the Caribbeans The Thompson Twin's believe that technologies are emerging and affecting our lives in ways that indicate we are at the beginning of a Fourth Industrial Revolution. It is, therefore, worthwhile taking some time to consider precisely what kind of shifts we are experiencing and how we might, collectively and individually, ensure that it creates benefits for the many. While a market economy has many advantages, such as fostering innovation, variety, and individual choice, it also has disadvantages, such as a tendency for an inequitable distribution of wealth and income for the many. The U.S. consumer spending represents 65 to 70 percent of GDP buying power in the U.S. economy. This is the underlying reason to create and maintain jobs to support the American consumer. "No Consumer - No Economy."